NED MANNING is a writer, actor and teacher. He has written many plays for adults and young people. Among his published plays are *Us or Them*, *Milo*, *Close to the Bone* and *Luck of the Draw* as well as short plays in the anthologies *Short Circuit* and *No Nudity, Weapons or Naked Flames*. Other plays for adults include *Kenny's Coming Home* and *Last One Standing*. His latest play, *Tsunami*, was shortlisted for the STC's Patrick White Award in 2015.

Ned's plays for young people include *Alice Dreaming*, *Gods of War*, *Women of Troy* (adapted from Euripides' original drama, *The Trojan Women*) and Shakespeare for Australian Schools. He was nominated for an AWGIE for *Romeo and Juliet Intensive*, a play for young people that moves between Shakespeare's world and contemporary Australia. The script was written for The Bell Shakespeare Company's Actors at Work program, and toured all over Australia.

His radio adaptation of *Women of Troy* was nominated for the Prix Marulic Festival of Radio Drama in Croatia in 2013. Ned's first work of nonfiction, *Playground Duty*, is a celebration of the teaching profession and a survival guide for young teachers.

As an actor, Ned has appeared in some of Australia's most loved film, television and theatre productions including: *Looking for Alibrandi*, *Offspring*, *The Shiralee*, *Bodyline* and *Aftershocks*. He starred in the 1980's cult classic *Dead End Drive-In*. His latest appearance was in the 2014 feature film, *The Menkoff Method*.

Ned has worked as a teacher and dramaturg, designing playwriting courses for youth and adults. He is committed to working with playwrights of all ages and providing them with support and professional guidance.

SHANE MCNAMARA is a professional actor and songwriter. He released his first album, 'Nasty Habit', in the mid-eighties and has subsequently performed on numerous albums in his role of Rat in a Hat in the children's series 'Bananas in Pyjamas'. He also penned the hit 'Banana Holiday'. *Kenny's Coming Home* was his first fully staged musical..

Rebecca Hickey as Kim in Q Theatre's 1991 production. (Photo: Q Theatre)

KENNY'S COMING HOME

NED MANNING
WITH MUSIC AND LYRICS BY SHANE McNAMARA

Currency Press • Sydney

CURRENCY PLAYS

First published in 2016
by Currency Press Pty Ltd,
PO Box 2287, Strawberry Hills, NSW, 2012, Australia
enquiries@currency.com.au
www.currency.com.au

Copyright: *Kenny's Coming Home* © Ned Manning & Shane McNamara, 1991, 2016.

COPYING FOR EDUCATIONAL PURPOSES

The Australian *Copyright Act 1968* (Act) allows a maximum of one chapter or 10% of this book, whichever is the greater, to be copied by any educational institution for its educational purposes provided that that educational institution (or the body that administers it) has given a remuneration notice to Copyright Agency Limited (CAL) under the Act.
For details of the CAL licence for educational institutions contact CAL, 11/66 Goulburn Street, Sydney, NSW, 2000; tel: within Australia 1800 066 844 toll free; outside Australia 61 2 9394 7600; fax: 61 2 9394 7601; email: info@copyright.com.au

COPYING FOR OTHER PURPOSES

Except as permitted under the Act, for example a fair dealing for the purposes of study, research, criticism or review, no part of this book may be reproduced, stored in a retrieval system, or transmitted in any form or by any means without prior written permission. All enquiries should be made to the publisher at the address above.

Any performance or public reading of *Kenny's Coming Home* is forbidden unless a licence has been received from the authors or the authors' agent. The purchase of this book in no way gives the purchaser the right to perform the play in public, whether by means of a staged production or a reading. All applications for public performance should be addressed to RGM Artist Group, PO Box 128, Surry Hills NSW 2010, Australia; ph: 61 2 9281 3911; email: info@rgm.com.au

Cataloguing-in-publication data for this title is available from the National Library of Australia website: www.nla.gov.au

Typeset by Dean Nottle for Currency Press.
Cover design by Katy Wall for Currency Press.
Front cover shows Melissa Jaffer as Aunt Dorothy and Duncan Wass as Dad in the 1991 Q Theatre production.

Currency Press acknowledges the Traditional Owners of the Country on which we live and work. We pay our respects to all Aboriginal and Torres Strait Islander Elders, past and present.

Contents

KENNY'S COMING HOME
    Act One   1
    Act Two   33

Duncan Wass as Dad and Melissa Jaffer as Aunt Dorothy in Q Theatre's 1991 production. (Photo: Q Theatre)

Kenny's Coming Home was first produced by Q Theatre, Penrith, on 16 November 1991, with the following cast:

MUM	Michelle Fawdon
AUNT DOROTHY	Melissa Jaffer
KENNY	David James
KIM	Rebecca Hickey
DAD	Duncan Wass

Director, Helmut Bakaitis
Designer, Judith Hoddinott
Lighting designer, Bruce McKendry
Choreography, Geoffrey Jenkins

CHARACTERS

KIM
A.D. (AUNT DOROTHY), Dad's elder sister
MUM
DAD
KENNY

SETTING

Penrith 1990. A suburban home, modestly decorated. A TV set is prominent. The set is dominated by trophies, photos and memorabilia from the Penrith Panthers Golden Years. Son Kenny is prominent in these. Alongside them, in a position which in another time we may have seen a photograph of the queen, is a photograph of Ben Chifley. The house then, is a shrine to the Penrith Panthers and the Australian Labor Party, with the TV running a near third.

The other major features are a window that opens to the vegetable garden, a door that leads to the kitchen and a door to the outside world.

ACT ONE

SCENE ONE

During the opening song montages are established of KIM *with a schoolbag,* MUM *doing domestics,* DAD *watering the garden and* A.D. *having a drink.*

SONG: 'MONDAY TO SUNDAY'

KIM: Jesus, what a bloody day it's so hot
 Garden looks as though it's going to rot
 God I wish I was still in Balmain
 Diving into the swimming pool again
 Or take a bus down to the beach
 Living in the west it seems out of reach

A.D.: Jesus, bugger of a day it's so hot
 Garden looks as though it's going to rot
 God I wish I was still in Balmain
 Chatting with Flo across the lane
 Taking a train into the city
 Compared to here it was bloody pretty

ALL: [*Chorus*] Monday seems to be a lot like Friday
 Sunday mustn't be confused with Tuesday
 Wednesday just hangs about
 Thursday I've got my doubts
 Saturday well it's not too bad
 And there you go that's the week I've had

ALL: What are we gonna do?
 The choices here are few
 What's to do, what's to do?

KIM: When

ALL: [*Chorus*] Monday seems to be a lot like Friday
 Sunday mustn't be confused with Tuesday

Wednesday just hangs about
Thursday I've got my doubts
Saturday well it's not too bad
And there you go that's the week I've had

MUM & KIM: [*Chorus*] Monday seems to be a lot like Friday
Sunday mustn't be confused with Tuesday
Wednesday just hangs about
Thursday I've got my doubts
Saturday well it's not too bad
And there you go that's the week I've had

DAD & A.D.: [*sung simultaneously with above chorus*]
Every day's the same
Every day's the same
Every day's the same.

They disappear as the song ends.

Lighting change. Late afternoon.

A schoolbag flies through the window, followed by KIM. *She is a confident teenager with a worldly wisdom that belies her years. She addresses the audience, lighting a cigarette as she does so.*

KIM: Hi! Pretty hot, eh? I tell ya, the winds out here are a killer. Mind you, they're nothing here compared to Mount Druitt, they really sort you out. My name's Kim.

Kim Green. Year Twelve Penrith High, school vice-captain, hockey rep, average student, so Mr Gould says, but what would he know? He only says that because he's the football coach. The only reason he pays me any attention at all is because I'm Kenny's sister and as everyone with half a brain knows, Kenny was one of the best footballers the Panthers ever had.

My brother Kenny is what you call a legend. You don't have to be dead to be a legend, as long as you've played for the mighty Penrith Panthers. Kenny won more trophies than most of you have had hot dinners. He was there as the club began its rise from the ashes, leading from the front, never taking a backward step and all those other clichés.

ACT ONE

He led the side into the play-off with Balmain in eighty-eight, where we were robbed, and promptly retired.

'Work commitments'. Oh yeah, piss-weak excuse. I reckon Irene put the pressure on him.

I tell ya, woudda brought a tear to his eyes to see the boys' fantastic win this year, 'specially with his old mate Roycie scoring a couple of meat pies.

Anyway, eventually he pissed off, to Adelaide. Adelaide! I mean, they don't even play footy there, just Aussie Rules. I tell you, Dad still hasn't recovered. He reckoned Kenny was a future MP for sure, especially if he captained the Panthers to a premiership win.

We used to live in Balmain, before the trendies moved in. We lived in a cottage near Dawn Fraser's pool, but then some yuppie management consultants offered us so much money for the place we couldn't refuse. A.D. was horrified, but Dad saw it as a good career move both workwise and politically. You see Dad always fantasised about becoming a politician, reckons Granddad wanted one of his family to go into parliament.

Dad goes to political meetings all the time. Gee, I reckon Mum still misses her mates in Balmain, and her job. A.D. did, till she discovered bingo at Panthers.

We used to have singalong. Mum sang all these really daggy songs, like:

'She wore an itsy bitsy teeny weeny
Yellow polka dot bikini …'

God! Sexist or what! And rave, Mum used to rave about Johnny O'Keefe and Elvis the Pelvis. Dad loved Herman's Hermits, whoever they were. Kenny was into heavy metal and Bobby Fulton, even though he played for Manly. Uggh! Deep Purple. You know …

She performs a few bars of a Deep Purple classic.

He had a poster of Suzi Quatro hanging above his bed. I caught him wanking over her one night and bribed a packet of Winnie Blues outta him. Told him I'd tell his girlfriend. Wouldn't do now he's a partner in an architectural firm. One of Adelaide's most progressive Irene reckons. Trendies!

AUNT DOROTHY *enters.*

A.D.: Hello, Kim darling. School over already?

KIM: Yes. Hi, A.D, thought I'd get a bit of homework done. Trials are coming up soon.

A.D.: That's a good girl.

She peers out the window.

Yes, the sun's over the yardarm, time for a little snifter.

She helps herself to a generous brandy.

Hot, isn't it, dear? You know, I still haven't got used to being away from the harbour breeze.

She turns on a little propeller-like fan and holds it close to her face.

So, what are you studying now?

KIM: Australian History. We're doing all that stuff about de Groot and Jack Lang.

Must've been pretty wild, de Groot galloping across the Bridge like that, bet the old stuffed shirts got a bit of a shock!

A.D.: De Groot, my dear, was a fascist, member of an organisation called the New Guard.

KIM: Yeah, I know.

A.D.: I hope they're telling history like it was, not through rose-coloured glasses. Life was pretty tough for the working class in those days, you know. At least Jack Lang had his heart in the right place, at least he was a Labor man. Ironical that Keating should hero-worship him.

KIM: Yeah.

A.D.: You know, in my day the Labor Party wouldn't have dreamt of protecting these white collar criminals like they do today. I tell you bloody what, if I had my way people like Bond and Elliott would be behind bars. And I'd throw away the keys.

KIM: Yeah, yeah.

A.D.: If it wasn't for the Liberals being the born-to-rule leeches that they are, I'd have abandoned the Labor Party years ago.

KIM: Yes, well I better get to work, A.D. … a girl's gotta do what a girl's gotta do.

A.D.: Hey, Kim, come here. Ask your teacher about the formation of the DLP.

ACT ONE

KIM: What?

A.D.: Ask your teacher why the DLP was formed. When he tells you if it was a right-wing movement you tell him he's wrong. You tell him it was formed as a left-wing movement before it was taken over by the Catholic right. That'll stump him.

KIM: Her.

A.D.: Eh?

KIM: Her, Miss Eddington is a *her*. See ya, A.D.

KIM exits to do her homework.

A.D.: Eddington. Was that the fellow who formed BHP? No, I think that might have been Essington something. Ah-ha! Might just slip down for a quiet beer before the branch meeting. Need something to liven this place up a bit, can't even get a good argument anymore. God love you, Chif.

She exits, saluting the picture of Ben Chifley as she goes.

KIM runs in and grabs a portable radio. She turns it on.

RADIO: Here is a quick newsflash. The Member for Penrith, Derek Brennan, has had a heart attack playing squash. His condition is believed to be critical. This is bad news for the Labor government as a by-election is the last thing they need, even if the seat is one of the safest Labor seats in the country.

This is radio 2KA, playing hot hits and favourites.

The radio plays something wildly inappropriate.

KIM: [*exiting*] Sensitively handled.

SCENE TWO

MUM *enters, carrying groceries.*
She sings to the TV.

SONG: *'BOREDOM AFTER TEA'*

MUM: Good Lord, that's better
Oh dear what a day
Traffic, unbelievable
Oh that's a nice frock

Yes, Kim would look
So nice in one of those
Oh no, he's ugly, got such a pointy nose

And here I sit watchin' the TV
Oh it's five p.m. Dad'll be on the train about now
Better get the tea on. About now
Better get the tea on

Oh no, not him
God woman, where's your taste?
That's right, I agree
Should do something 'bout her hair though
Looks silly, looks ridiculous
Looks a bit like mine really
Oh no, the one in blue, he's more the one for you

And here I sit watchin' the TV
Oh it's five p.m. Dad'll be on the train about now

MUM *is joined by voices from offstage:*

ALL: Better get the tea on. About now
Better get the tea on

ALL: [*Chorus*] At times I think of life without TV
And all I see is boredom after tea
Game shows, movies, it all pleases me
Saves me from the boredom after tea
Saves me from the boredom after tea

MUM: Oh no, he's ugly, got such a pointy nose
That's new, looks good, must be better than mine
And that girl, lovely teeth
I've seen her somewhere before
That's right, in that soap, she was the prostitute
She was good, did all the covers
Wonder what happened to her?

ALL: [*Chorus*] At times I think of life without TV
And all I see is boredom after tea
Game shows, movies, it all pleases me

ACT ONE

    Boredom after tea
    Saves me from the boredom after tea
    Saves me from the boredom after tea.

MUM dozes off. The song has constituted a passage of time.

KIM enters and addresses MUM.

KIM: Mum! Mum, are you with us?
MUM: Eh? Oh, you're home already, I was just watching …
KIM: Any specials?
MUM: Ooh. It's still hot, isn't it? Wish it'd rain.
KIM: Shit, Mum, the ice-cream's melted! Yuk!

She licks the ice-cream with her finger. MUM *watches TV.*

Wanna lick?
MUM: Oh no, I've missed 'Empty Boxes'.
KIM: Carn, Mum, have a finger.
MUM: Grab us a pen, dear. I tried that stuff and it didn't make the sheets any whiter, made them greyer if anything. This is a story for 'The Investigators', just the sort of thing Helen Wellings could get her teeth into.

KIM hands MUM pen and paper, still licking the ice-cream and now mesmerised by the TV.

It's high time these charlatans were exposed. There you go, another one. How on earth can one sanitary pad be softer than another, look at that girl!
KIM: I never feel like that when I get a period.
MUM: False advertising.
KIM: I like this show.
MUM: It occurred to me today that shopping just isn't the fun it used to be. I mean, when we lived in Balmain you could have a bit of a chat, wander about. The girls in the supermarket here are either dead or they bite your head off.
KIM: I like Darryl Somers, he's cute.
MUM: Graham Kennedy used to do that show, it was funnier then.
KIM: Like a cuppa? Mum?
MUM: Love one.
KIM: Can I scab a fag?

MUM: I suppose so, don't tell Dad.
KIM: I'll put the shopping away.
MUM: You after something?
KIM: Mum!

    KIM *takes a cigarette, then another, and exits with the shopping.*

MUM: If that's cute, I'll give up. Toe! Must be, can't be anything else. Mmm, I suppose it could be head. Perhaps it's foot. Clive was angry with Claude when he dropped a brick on his 'blank'. Has to be toe.
KIM: [*off*] Did you hear that Mr Brennan dropped dead playing squash?
MUM: Quick, dear.
KIM: [*off*] Dad'll be upset.
MUM: Here!

    KIM *rushes in.*

KIM: What?
MUM: What do you think, dear?
KIM: About what?
MUM: This. 'Clive was angry with Claude when he dropped a brick on his …' I reckon it's toe. Has to be.
KIM: Bananas.
MUM: Very funny.
KIM: Did you hear …?
MUM: Here we go. Toe, foot, toe, head, head, head. Well well, there you go.
KIM: What's this?

    She picks up a parcel.

MUM: What? Oh, that. You weren't meant to see that. It's a surprise.
KIM: For me?
MUM: Well, it's not for Kenny, is it?
KIM: Thanks, Mum.

    She tears open the parcel, revealing a Johnny O'Keefe album.

Johnny O'Keefe? Who's he when he's at home?
MUM: Just the greatest singer this country ever produced.
KIM: God! Look at the clothes.
MUM: The Wild One.
KIM: Nineteen fifty-seven! You're kidding.

ACT ONE

MUM: Thanks, Mum.
KIM: Oh, no, I mean it's great. Really. It's a lovely surprise.
MUM: Well, I thought seeing as you're so keen on dancing, I thought I might show you a few of the songs I used to know and maybe a few of the dances ... you know, if you're interested.
KIM: Sure, Mum, that'd be great.

>MUM *sings 'Six O'Clock Rock' and begins to dance.*
>
>*As she is transported into her past,* KIM *addresses the audience.*

That's my mum. How embarrassing. I mean, how do you deal with parents? I never thought she'd settle in here after we left Balmain. She kinda has, though. Anyway, I like Penrith. The people are real out here. I'm glad we left Balmain ... there's only so many trendoids one person can stand. You know they didn't even have a Labor Member there for a while. Can you believe that, it's the birthplace of the Labor Party too. Anyway, it'll be unrecognisable soon, once the developers finish with it. A.D. reckons the Labor Party isn't true to its roots anymore. I suppose she'd know; she's been a member for nearly fifty years. We're all members. It's great at branch meetings when Dad and A.D. get stuck into each other. Mum mediates, she often takes the minutes. I'm one of the youngest members in our branch. I took Spud, my ex, but he got bored. Got the concentration span of a gnat. That's why he's my ex.

>MUM *snaps out of her dancing, JO'K has taken her to another place.*

MUM: There's some great music here, Kim. Your dad and me used to jive to this. I'll show you how.

>*She does, singing joyfully, as she shows* KIM *how to jive.*

Not bad. You know, I saw Johnny O'Keefe at the Stadium. I must have been twelve or maybe thirteen. We caught the tram all the way up William Street, over the hill at the Cross, then down the other side to the Stadium.

It was fantastic. My first concert. Mum and Dad thought we were going to the pictures. We wore our hair in a bun with a ponytail. I had bobby socks and the tightest jumper I could find. We screamed and yelled and then, out he came. Dolores Poppadopalos fainted, dropped like a sack of wheat. We didn't take too much notice of poor Dolores. We were there to see the Wild One, our hero, Johnny O'Keefe. He was out of this world. He wore the tightest trousers, he bulged and our imaginations went wild. We twisted, we shouted, we sweated until the sweat was dripping off us. He stuck out his crutch and wiggled his bottom and we roared ourselves hoarse. I was on another planet and I loved it. I thought I'd burst. That night, I lay in bed and my ears were ringing and my body was still shaking. I was deliriously happy. I loved Johnny O'Keefe.

DAD *bursts in. He rushes to the phone, indicates to turn the TV down, and speaks.* MUM *sits with* KIM *and they both watch TV.*

DAD: [*on the phone*] Rod? Yes, you've heard? Dropped dead playing squash. I know. I told him to watch his weight. And the drink, Christ his cholesterol level was up to buggery, but he wouldn't exercise and the stupid bugger wouldn't listen. That's right, son. Yeah. It's a tragedy, but we can't let the grass grow, can we? I mean, we've got a party to run and, for all his faults, Derek would've wanted us to carry on. He wouldn't have wanted us to lose any ground by crying over spilt milk, if you know what I mean. Son, we've got a candidate to choose and a by-election to win. I know we'll win it, but we don't want a big swing again as it'll look bad for the party. Okay. Oh yes, I know, it's very sad indeed. Talk soon. 'Bye.

He hangs up.

Bloody pissant.

MUM: I'm writing to Consumer Affairs, false advertising leads to false expectations.

DAD: You heard about Derek?

MUM: Derek?

DAD: Dropped dead playing squash.

MUM: Poor Cynthia.

KIM: Poor Derek, he's the dead one.

DAD: Couldn't have happened at a worse time for the party.

MUM: She won't know what to do with herself without all those functions to attend.

DAD: This is, of course, an opportunity for the party to pick a candidate more in touch with—

ACT ONE

KIM: The people?

DAD: With the economic climate. Poor Derek, bless his soul, was like your aunt, thought the Whitlam fiasco was a success.

MUM: Well, to a certain extent, it was.

DAD: Yeah, just ask Malcolm Fraser.

MUM: I'd say recognising that China existed wasn't a bad start.

DAD: Bloody hot, eh? Drying the garden out.

MUM: Not to mention Vietnam.

    DAD *goes to the window and looks out.*

DAD: Damn and blast! That rotten dog's been into the garden again.

    DAD *climbs out the window.*

MUM: What?

DAD: My zucchinis!

SONG: *'THE ZUCCHINI SONG'*

DAD: Some people think that it's so easy
           To grow the perfect zucchini
           Oh it needs a lot of love 'n' care 'n' attention
           Needs a lot of love in another dimension

           Mix it up with garlic
           And a touch of onion
           Thinly sliced and a pinch of cinnamon

           Zucchini

           My mangled friend, I am so sorry
           The perfect proof of watering poorly
           Never gave enough love 'n' care 'n' attention
           Never gave enough love in another dimension
           Just enough water and just enough sunshine
           Just enough love to create the perfect vine

DAD: [*Chorus*] And every seed I plant
           And every inch you grow
           Every sprout that shows
           With every garden hose
           I'll be watching you

MUM & KIM: [*Chorus*] Every seed I plant
DAD: Every inch you grow
MUM & KIM: Every inch you grow
ALL: I'll be watching you.

> A.D. *enters, wheeling a shopping trolley. If possible, she should have a dog inside, along with a few cartons of beer and a carton of Craven A cigarettes. She has had a beer or two.*

A.D.: Evening, all. Bad luck about Derek, eh? Maybe they'll get someone with enough guts to stand up to the economic bloody rationalists. You know who I'd like to see stand, don't ya? Kenny.

MUM: Kenny?

A.D.: Be ideal. Young, popular, charismatic, enough mongrel.

KIM: Kenny's in Adelaide, A.D.

A.D.: So? Adelaide isn't another planet, is it?

MUM: I think he's quite happy where he is.

KIM: God knows why, married to that tightarse.

MUM: Kim!

KIM: Well, she is. Bloody North Shore snob.

MUM: Kenny's happy, that's all that matters.

KIM: If that's what it takes to be happy I'd rather be dead.

A.D.: What's Artie doing?

> DAD *appears at the window with an armful of zucchinis.*

DAD: Here, shove them in the fridge, they'll perish in this heat.

A.D.: Artie! You'll ruin your good suit. What'll the neighbours think?

> DAD *has a quick, paranoid look around.*

DAD: No-one's around, are they?

MUM: No, dear.

DAD: Here. That's the last of them. If I catch that dog, it's dead meat.

A.D.: Dead meat! Who are you kidding?

DAD: I mean it.

A.D.: Yeah, yeah.

> *She exists, whistling, with shopping trolley.*

DAD: Therefore, before our very eyes, goes an example of the living dead. Well, what about Derek, eh?

MUM: What about Derek?

ACT ONE

DAD: Well, you know.
MUM: No.
KIM: I think I know what's coming up.
DAD: How'd you like a spell in Canberra?
MUM: Canberra?
DAD: The national capital.
KIM: I thought as much.
MUM: Canberra? I could think of nothing worse.
DAD: Hey. Come on now. It's a beautiful city, beautifully planned, marvellous facilities …
KIM: They've got a party called 'The Sun Ripened Tomato Party'.
DAD: Kim, please.
KIM: They have, they've also got a 'Party That Doesn't Want To Be A Party'.
MUM: Bureaucracy gone mad!
KIM: And they've got the biggest, most inefficient local government in the history of the universe.
MUM: And the highest suicide rate.
DAD: And the national parliament. Reckon you might soon change your mind as the wife of the Member for Lindsay.
MUM: You're joking.
DAD: Never been more serious in my life.
MUM: You might have got me to move out here, but Canberra?
DAD: Come on, don't you see? It's all falling into place.
KIM: I told you.
DAD: I mean, I feel terrible about Derek, but the fact of the matter is that he wasn't cutting the mustard. Chances are he would have been replaced before the next election anyway. He didn't understand the need for change. Too hidebound by dogma. We have to be flexible as a party. We need to sniff out what the electorate wants and give it to them. No-one gives a stuff about social change. What we've got to do is maintain that middle ground.
KIM: Don't let A.D. hear you say that.
DAD: Your aunt is a dinosaur.
KIM: I think I'm going to spew.
DAD: Now hang on. I might as well lay my cards on the table.

    A.D. *enters.*

A.D.: Who's for a drink?
DAD: Dorothy, I've got something to say to the whole family.
A.D.: Will I need a strong one?
KIM: A double, I'd say.
DAD: I have decided, after careful consideration, to throw my hat into the ring.
A.D.: He's joining the circus.
MUM: I think so.
DAD: You all know that there has always been a desire in the family to serve the Labor Party in any way we can. To answer the call, so to speak. Well, I believe the call has come. I want you to know that I make this decision with the best interests of the party at heart.
A.D.: The poor bugger's still warm in his grave and already you're jumping into his shoes.
DAD: I am going to need your support, your understanding and your patience. I'm going to ring Kenny. He could play a vital part in the campaign. I reckon with him on board, I'll be damn near unbeatable. Imagine the publicity he'll bring.
KIM: Kenny's in Adelaide, Dad.
DAD: He can take a couple of weeks off.
MUM: Yes, well …
DAD: It's all settled then.
A.D.: I don't believe my ears are hearing this.
DAD: Come on, Dot, this is what Dad always dreamt of, this is why we moved out here, this is the chance of a lifetime. Well?

A stunned silence.

I knew you'd all agree. Ha, ha! I suppose I'd better do something about that garden, can't have the candidate setting a bad example.

SCENE THREE

KIM *is setting the table. The ritualised evening meal. TV competes for attention.* MUM *is preparing dinner in the kitchen.*

KIM: Get on to Kenny, Mum?

MUM *enters with food.*

MUM: No, Irene was very evasive. Said he'd gone away on business.

ACT ONE

KIM: She said that last time.
MUM: I know. Jeremy sounded tense last time I spoke to him. Maybe business is bad.
KIM: We are in a recession, Mum.
MUM: I suppose. Knowing Kenny, he's probably got his nose to the grindstone. Working his way out of trouble, that'd be his way.
KIM: Yeah, just like he played footy, head down, arse up.
MUM: Hey! Kenny wasn't a grafter, he had class, a Rolls Royce, like Brandy.
KIM: Yeah, Brandy …
MUM: He was a beautiful baby.
KIM: Brandy?
MUM: No, Kenny! Although I'm sure Brandy was a beautiful baby too.
KIM: Wouldn't have minded changing his nappies …
MUM: He was no trouble, slept like a top, good feeder, bit of a dream, really.

The TV wins KIM*'s attention.*

KIM: What's this?
MUM: I do miss him.

A.D. *enters as* KIM *is transfixed by the TV.*

What a lot of crap.
A.D.: TV was invented to transmit crap.
KIM: Never trust a politician, eh?
A.D.: Absolutely not.
KIM: Is he Labor or Liberal?
A.D.: Hard to tell.
KIM: Boring.
A.D.: Insincere.
KIM: God, he's up himself.
A.D.: Job requirement. Your dad should do well.
KIM: Lost me.
A.D.: If your father wins preselection, I'm going to move out.
KIM: Why?
A.D.: I couldn't stand it. Bad enough leaving Balmain without having to take part in the destruction of a great party.
KIM: What? Dad?

A.D.: Wouldn't know a working man if he fell over one. Not anymore. God, I can still remember the day he was born. What a racket! Should have known then he'd cause trouble.

    DAD *enters, ready for dinner.*

DAD: Who?
A.D.: You.
DAD: What? I mean, beg your pardon?
A.D.: You always caused trouble.
DAD: Oh, really? Dinner ready?
MUM: [*off*] Nearly.
DAD: Better check the hose. Back in five.

    He exits.

KIM: What was Dad like as a kid?
A.D.: Alright. He was always ambitious. Sold papers at the cricket, mowed lawns, anything for a quid. Always upwardly mobile. Pretended to live in Drummoyne, used to put on the dog like your Uncle Wally does when he's on the slops. I used to laugh at him. Well, look at him now. Obsessive.

    They watch DAD *out the window.*

KIM: What was he like at school?
A.D.: Sat up the front.
KIM: Uh-huh.
A.D.: Good footy player, though. Smack in the mouth usually got him going. Then you saw the real Artie, a scrapper. If only the opposition knew, they'd have left him alone. He played like a demon when he was riled. I remember one day this bloke from Souths belted him and a brawl broke out. It was at Leichhardt.

    This bird brain on the hill gets stuck into Artie, so I gave her a bit of lip. She spat the dummy and before I knew where we were, it was on. Top day, it was. You wouldn't think so to look at him now, but he could go a bit, your old man. He looked out for me when Bert took off with that tart from Annandale. Swore he'd kill Bert if he ever saw him again.

    MUM *enters, carrying dinner.*

MUM: Don't mind me, I only work here.

ACT ONE

KIM: Oh, sorry, Mum.
MUM: That's okay, dear, you can clean up, if you can manage, that is.
A.D.: My fault, love, reminiscing.
MUM: Again.
A.D.: Fair go.

    DAD *enters.*

DAD: Good, I'm starving.

    He changes the TV channel.

'7.30 Report'. Good.
A.D.: Tea looks good.
DAD: Oh, they're onto the new housing project. Typical greenies. Live in fairyland.
KIM: They're not gonna put houses there, are they?
DAD: Bloody interest groups.
A.D.: That shady mate of yours is involved in that, isn't he?
DAD: Bloody hell, I thought we left the basket weavers in Balmain.
A.D.: You know, Artie, that bloke who misappropriated all that money from council.
MUM: Edgar Brit.
A.D.: That's him.
KIM: What a load of bull.
DAD: Kim! You're going to have to watch your language, young lady.
KIM: What a sleazebag.
MUM: He's a developer, darling.
A.D.: Drive you to drink.

    A.D. *gets herself a drink.*

DAD: Pass the choko pickle please, Kim. Well, it's pretty simple. If you don't build houses, where are people going to live? Someone's going to make a quid out of it, but that's progress.
A.D.: The 'someone' is probably on Council, or maybe even in a political party.
MUM: Or maybe even standing for preselection.
DAD: Typically trendy argument which ignores economic reality.
KIM: Hey, what's the story with Chif, A.D?
A.D.: Didn't I tell you?

KIM: Nuh.
DAD: No.
KIM: What?
DAD: No. Not nuh, no.
A.D.: Pedant. Well, anyway, you know how he was staying with Roger and Beryl.
DAD: Lucky Chif.
A.D.: If you'd finished the birdcage for me when I asked, I wouldn't have had to bother.
DAD: Sorry!
A.D.: Well, Beryl put Chif in the laundry.
KIM: And?
A.D.: Well, idiot Roger forgot to lock the door.
KIM: What, and Chif took off?
A.D.: No. Their rotten mongrel cat got into the laundry.
KIM: Oh, no.
A.D.: It must have opened the cage.
KIM: No!
A.D.: I was in the kitchen when I heard this God-almighty noise goin' on. The next thing I know, there's this bloody cat tearing around the place, with Chif firmly wedged between its fangs.

    Feathers everywhere. I threw a picture at it, actually it was one of you playing football, Artie. Hit it too, but the bloody thing shot through.
KIM: Is Chif alright?
A.D.: Alright? How would you like to be dragged around the place by a bloody lion or something? I put the poor little bugger back on his perch, but he just fell off. Shock, I reckon.
KIM: Dead?
A.D.: As a dodo.
MUM: What happened to the cat?
A.D.: When it came back, I grabbed hold of it and drop-kicked it over the fence. Beryl got the shits.
DAD: What's the cat's name? Ming.

    DAD *falls about at his joke,* MUM *smiles surreptitiously.*

A.D.: Very funny.

ACT ONE

KIM: What's the joke?
DAD: Chif ... Ming ... don't you see?
    DAD *returns his focus to the TV.*
KIM: No.
A.D.: Chifley ... Menzies. Menzies beat Chifley, bank nationalisation. Red scare.
KIM: Oh.
A.D.: Come on, let's clear the table.

SONG: 'OH, WHAT FUN'

DAD:	I've been thinking dear
MUM:	Who you calling dear?
DAD:	It's something kinda fun
MUM:	I could do with some ... round here
DAD:	We could hold a bash
MUM:	We haven't got the cash
DAD:	I thought we'd have it here
MUM:	Oh, did you really, dear ... oh, what fun
DAD:	[*Chorus*] Nothing too fancy, just a barbeque
Couple of beers, a bit of salad too
The family man at home
Could be worth a vote or two
And we could have it here on Saturday night
I'll make out a list of who to invite, tonight
We're gonna have a party on Saturday night
Around the Hills hoist we'll put up the lights
Alright. Alright?
KIM:	Could I have Channel Ten?
A.D.:	Have we got any wine?
DAD:	You could bring a friend
MUM:	Oh, how very kind ... can't wait
KIM:	What's he on about?
A.D.:	I don't want to know
MUM:	A knees-up Mother Brown
A.D.:	For all his Labor Joes

ALL: Oh what fun

DAD: [*Chorus*] Nothing too fancy, just a barbeque
Couple of beers, a bit of salad too
The family man at home
Could be worth a vote or two
And we could have it here on Saturday night
I'll make out a list of who to invite, tonight

ALL: We're gonna have a party on Saturday night
Around the Hills hoist we'll put up the lights
Alright. Alright?
We're gonna have a party on Saturday night
Around the Hills hoist we'll put up the lights
Alright. Alright?

DAD: You know, I was thinking …
A.D.: That's a first.
DAD: They make a lot of sense, these economists.
MUM: Economic rationalists, you mean.
DAD: What he's saying is true, we have to find our feet in the marketplace.
A.D.: Give me a break.
DAD: There is no point in supporting outmoded work practices.
A.D.: You're talking like a management consultant.
DAD: These are hard times, and they call for disciplined measures.
A.D.: Yes, just ask the banks, they showed a lot of discipline, didn't they?
DAD: Don't be bloody ridiculous.
KIM: You're going to have to watch your language, young man!
A.D.: What happened to the Australian Labor Party, eh? Labor.
DAD: Something really stupid happened, they decided it was better to be in Government rather than Opposition.
A.D.: All the bloody same, shop dummies with blow-waved hair and images instead of policies.
DAD: Yes, Dot.
A.D.: You'd appeal to Hewson; you should be standing for the Liberals.
DAD: Don't be so naive, politics is a game of balance.
A.D.: I'm sick of you! How can you have the nerve to stand for preselection when you don't believe in anything? Who's to represent the

ACT ONE

working man, eh? Some yuppie lawyer who's never seen a shovel in his life, and who's made a killing by forcing the working man out of the suburb he was born in.

DAD: Hang on, Dot!

A.D.: No, you hang on. It gives me the shits. These damn whiz-kids have no concern for the ordinary Australian. They do deals with Packer and allow the Bonds and Skases to rape the country. They form policies from their opinion polls. They have no respect for this country, or its traditions. They trade on the name of Labor. They're not interested in anyone but themselves.

DAD: I resent that!

A.D.: Tough titty!

DAD: Act your age.

A.D.: Don't you bloody well patronise me.

DAD: If you're so smart, why don't you stand for preselection? Put your money where your mouth is.

A.D.: I might just do that.

DAD: Oh yeah, you couldn't stay sober long enough.

As A.D. *goes to clout him,* KIM *addresses the audience.*

During KIM's *speech, the rest of the family leave the stage.*

KIM: Just like the good old days! A real family blue. I haven't seen A.D. that stirred up in ages. Not since Kenny turned up with his Porsche and announced he was marrying that dope from the North Shore.

I mean, when A.D. found out Irene lived in Gordon, she nearly had a fit. It's the safest Liberal seat in NSW! I reckon Irene only went with Kenny because he was meant to be a hero. Well. Dad enlisted the support of this Denise piece. She calls herself a feminist on the one hand, and a numbers cruncher on the other. I reckon I know what she crunches, and it ain't numbers.

So, this Denise is meant to be organising Dad's campaign. Lobbying, all that stuff. She's always ringing him up. It's really weird, kinda like he's having it off or something, though I can't imagine anyone having it off with Dad … Anyway, Dad's been busier than a one-legged tap dancer.

SCENE FOUR

DAD *is talking earnestly on the phone.*

DAD: [*on the phone*] Tremendous, Denise, tremendous. Of course, the only reason I'm standing is to serve the electorate! Make it clear that my goal is to ensure that the party goes into the next election confident that this seat will be held with an increased majority. Yes. So, there's only Rodney Cuttlefish and that clown from the BLF. No problems. No. Can't see any other nominations coming in between now and then.

Yes, I'm going to call Marsho, he's always looking for labourers. If we get Danny Maloney's son a job, that'd be a favour he owes us. You're dead right, and that favour may well be preferences for you know who.

You'll stuff the Left if you let it slip that Cuttlefish was going to vote against the housing project. I know, not strictly, but you know how these rumours start. We'll bury him and the Left once and for all.

Door knock? Ah no, well, I've covered most of the members, thought I'd leave the rest till Kenny comes home.

I reckon having him with me won't hurt at all. Ha! That's right. The whole family are ticket holders and I took the precaution of getting a few mates to join and attend the prerequisite number of meetings, so I reckon we're travelling pretty nicely. Yes. Listen, before you do, I just want say how grateful I am for your support and your encouragement, Denise. The dream's within our grasp.

God, I well remember the youthful euphoria of the Whitlam years. Thank God we listened to Hawkie, eh, and didn't maintain the rage. Thank God we saw the light, and, if you don't mind me saying so, Denise, thank God for you. Tonight? Of course, I'd be delighted.

> MUM *enters on the tail end of this conversation. She pays no attention to* DAD, *but his manner suddenly becomes conspiratorial.*

Uh ... yes, of course. Thank you. I'll see you tonight then.

> *He hangs up.*

ACT ONE

Um ... that was Marsho, he's got some people for me to meet. Influential. Better go. Won't be too late.
MUM: Seen my purse anywhere?
DAD: Par for the course, these meetings.
MUM: Oh, there it is.
DAD: You don't mind, do you?
MUM: What?
DAD: Right.
MUM: Come on, Dorothy, we'll be late.

> A.D. *races in, dressed to kill.*

A.D.: Panthers, here I come! I can smell a jackpot coming on, Kath.

> *They race off, virtually ignoring* DAD.

DAD: I, uh ... I won't be late.

SCENE FIVE

> MUM *and* A.D. *struggle in from a big night at the club, both carrying drinks. They are singing 'The Witch Doctor', dancing and generally having a good time, until* MUM *staggers and collapses in a chair.*

MUM: I'm going to be sick.
A.D.: No you're not.
MUM: Oh, yes I am.
A.D.: Hold onto it, Kath.

> *She plonks a bowl down in front of* MUM *and falls into a chair. A moment passes.*

MUM: He thinks I'm stupid. He thinks I don't have a brain.
A.D.: Who?
MUM: Your brother.
A.D.: Oh, him! The traitor. Judas of the Labor Party. The betrayer. The Vince Gair of the nineties!
MUM: That's the one.
A.D.: What do you think of the baldy chap I was chatting with?
MUM: Someone ought to take the wind out of his sails.
A.D.: I rather fancied him, meself.

MUM: Do you think he's having an affair?
A.D.: I don't know, I only met him tonight.
MUM: No, no. Arthur.
A.D.: Arthur? Who'd have an affair with Arthur? Oh, sorry love, wasn't having a go at you. I mean, he was alright … once.
MUM: That fellow with the terrible shirt, you know, he kept pestering me for a dance all night.
A.D.: Why didn't you?
MUM: I will, one of these days.
A.D.: Won't Artie poop himself then!
MUM: They said baldy men are more virile.
A.D.: Who does?
MUM: They do.
A.D.: Up the mighty Tigers!

> KIM *enters. She too has had a night on the town.*

MUM: Hello, dear.
KIM: Few quieties, eh, girls?
A.D.: Just a couple. Your wally.

> KIM *gets herself a drink.*

Have a small one yourself.
KIM: Where's the old man?
A.D.: Out.
KIM: As usual.
MUM: Campaigning. He's frantically trying to arrange numbers.
A.D.: That's why he got that group from the bowling club to join. God, that was months ago. Not as silly as he looks. He's been preparing for this for ages, hasn't he?
MUM: I'd say so.
KIM: How'd he know Derek was going to die?
MUM: He didn't, they were planning to give him the flick for ages.
A.D.: He saved them the trouble by carking it.
MUM: How's Spud, dear?
KIM: I told you, I dropped him. Can I scab a fag, Mum?
MUM: You shouldn't.
KIM: I've got a packet, anyway.
MUM: I bet you have.

ACT ONE

As KIM *fishes for a packet of cigarettes from her bag, a plastic bag full of dope drops out. A moment's silence.*

KIM: Oh, shit! Oh, this isn't mine. It's just. Um, it's not really what you think it is. God, I wonder how it got in my bag? Must have been that bloody Dingo. I don't know him all that well.

A.D.: Is that grass?

KIM: Grass? Um … just a little bit.

A.D.: Gis'a look.

KIM: I mean, I was getting a lift home with Dingo … you know what, he tried to get into my pants.

MUM: Oh no!

KIM: First time. God, boys are slack. That's it. He's finished. 'Specially now! This is going straight in the bin.

She goes to leave.

MUM: Hang on a tic.

KIM: Look, I'm really sorry, Mum. Please don't tell Dad.

MUM: I wouldn't mind trying some.

KIM: Wha … what?

MUM: Just once. I've heard so much about it.

KIM: Oh, come off it.

A.D.: Yes. Why not, you only live once.

MUM: Go on, dear, make us some.

KIM *hesitates, then expertly rolls a joint.*

This is a scientific experiment, nothing more. Better close the curtains.

She does, they smoke the joint. KIM *goes to the record player.*

KIM: Requests?

A.D.: Charlie Pride.

MUM: My throat's gone numb.

A.D.: Revolting smell.

KIM: I don't have Charlie Pride.

MUM: Jimmy Little.

A.D.: This won't have any effect on me. I could never be hypnotised, you know.

MUM: 'Royal Telephone'.

MUM *and* A.D. *sing a few bars of Jimmy Little's 'Royal Telephone'.*

KIM: Do you think Dad will win?
A.D.: Preselection? If he's organised the numbers.
MUM: He's got Denise doing that for him.
KIM: Um, Denise.
A.D.: Um, Denise.
MUM: Um, a mover and shaker.
KIM: Shit, what if he does win preselection?
A.D.: He's in Canberra. Not even the present Labor mob could lose this seat.
MUM: I don't know, Dot, they lost Newcastle.
A.D.: Ha! Crikey. I never thought of that, nothin's safe anymore.
MUM: What we need is a strong candidate.
A.D.: Yeah, Artie's too soft.
MUM: Remember Unsworth?
A.D.: And poor old Calwell.
MUM: *And* Bob.
A.D.: Bob who?
MUM: Hawke! 'We'll join the Push with Hawkie's George Bush.'
A.D.: No Australian blood will be spilt … until I get a phone call from George.
MUM: Dorothy?
A.D.: Yes?
MUM: Why, why don't you stand?
A.D.: Eh?
MUM: You'd be brilliant.
KIM: Yeah, A.D, excellent.
MUM: You've been a member long enough, you haven't missed a meeting in forty, I mean, thirty, years.
MUM / A.D.: [*together*] Twenty-five …
KIM: Yeah, A.D? Why not?
MUM: Think of 'The light on the hill', A.D.

SONG: *'HAIL A.D.'*

A.D.:   I'm not saying yes to this
        But I must admit it could be bliss
        To put the wind up you know who
        Is worth the risk

ACT ONE

MUM: You could be like all those kitchen appliances
A labour saver that's what you'd be

KIM: You know you'll have my full support
But don't dare have another snort
Before Dad walks through that door
Declaring war

MUM / A.D.: You're being a bore

ALL: [*Chorus*] So hail [hail] hail [hail] A.D.
Gonna be on my TV
I said hail [hail] hail [hail] A.D.
Gonna be on my TV screen, whoa oh, whoa oh

A.D.: If I go to Canberra to represent the ALP
I want you to know I'll always be overseas

KIM: That's the way to go A.D, but don't forget me
I wouldn't mind a trip to Spain or Italy

MUM: Responsibility, that's the word that you ignore
I don't mean to be a bore but that's what's in store

KIM / A.D.: You're being a bore

ALL: [*Chorus*] So hail [hail] hail [hail] A.D.
Gonna be on my TV
I said hail [hail] hail [hail] A.D.
Gonna be on my TV screen, whoa oh, whoa oh

MUM / KIM: A.D, A.D. for MP
A.D, A.D. for MP
A.D, A.D. for MP

ALL: [*Chorus*] So hail [hail] hail [hail] A.D.
Gonna be on my TV
I said hail [hail] hail [hail] A.D.
Gonna be on my TV screen, whoa oh, whoa oh
Gonna be on my TV screen, whoa oh oh
Gonna be on my TV screen, whoa oh oh
Gonna be on my TV screen, whoa oh oh
Hail.

SCENE SIX

The next day. MUM, *in surprisingly good shape, tidies up. She sings a few bars of 'Knock on Your Door'.*
DAD *enters.*

DAD: What a mess.
MUM: Pardon?
DAD: Oh, someone's made a hell of a mess in the garden. Probably one of you lot. What a disgraceful performance last night. Let alone the example you're setting our daughter, I can't imagine. What's got into you? Really and truly. As for that incense, or whatever you call it, the smell is appalling. We're going to have to ask Dorothy to leave, she's a terrible influence on you, let alone Kim. Do you have any idea what would happen if someone found out about your behaviour last night? Can you imagine what it would mean to my political career?
MUM: And where exactly were you?
DAD: What?
MUM: Where were you?
DAD: I was out, er, door knocking.
MUM: With Denise?
DAD: Who? Denise? Don't be silly, I hardly have anything to do with her. She just works for the party.
MUM: Oh, yeah.
DAD: Well, I did have a few drinks with the boys. Marsho, Roycie, and the Nancarrow lads. Sorry.
MUM: How thick do you think I am?
DAD: Don't be so silly. Dorothy has to go …

    A.D. *enters.*

A.D.: I beg your pardon?
DAD: You're a bad influence around here.
A.D.: Oh, am I?
DAD: Yes, I, I think it's time you found your own place.
A.D.: Listen, young Artie, I happen to own a considerable share in this joint. You threaten me, and I'll force a bloody sale.
DAD: Don't call me Artie, it's so … juvenile.

ACT ONE

A.D.: Artie Fadden. He was one of your mob.
DAD: He was a bloody conservative.
MUM: Touché.

A disgruntled DAD *turns on the TV.*

DAD: Hope I haven't missed 'Sunday'.
MUM: All nominations in for preselection?
DAD: Only three. Cuttlefish, Maloney and myself. I'd be glad if you'd consider the implications of your actions in light of the impending ballot and beyond, before you carry on as you did last night. Ahh, the PM. Sssh.
MUM: Nominations closed?
DAD: No. Tomorrow's the last day. Won't be any more though. Sssh.
A.D.: Who says?
DAD: My research in this is impeccable. Sssh. Hey, Dot, how would you like a holiday in Iraq?
A.D.: Charming.

DAD *finds this enormously funny.* KIM *enters.*

KIM: Morning, all.
DAD: Sssh.
KIM: How's Denise?
DAD: Quiet please, Kim. It's all economics, no-one gives a stuff about land, sea and air?
   These reporters are outrageous; of course modern science will be able to solve all these problems.
KIM: Hey, Dad, you're not having an affair, are you?
A.D.: He's trying to emulate Hawke in his youth, aren't you, Artie?
DAD: Have a bit of bloody common sense, woman. For God's sake. I've just about had enough of this nonsense. I happen to be well on my way to a seat in Canberra. Please treat the situation with the respect it deserves. A man can't even watch television in his own home.

He storms off in high dudgeon.

The lights fade. KIM *addresses the audience.*

KIM: So, there we were. Dad all set for Canberra, and Aunt Dorothy all set to upset the apple cart. Oh, the night on the wacky weed, A.D. and Mum ended up on the table delivering their maiden address to parliament. 'Doesn't have any effect', they kept saying. Tell you what, after seeing them, I'm gonna give the stuff a big miss myself. It's a bit of a worry. I rang Kenny to let him know the goss. But he still wasn't there. I don't know what's going on. Strange people, these architects.

SCENE SEVEN

DAD *rushes in to answer the phone, it is late afternoon.*

DAD: [*on the phone*] Hello? Oh, hello, Denise. Hang on a tic.

He checks that no-one is listening.

So, how's everything? All in readiness? Before you do, can I say just how much I enjoyed myself on Saturday night. Yes, yes, but I just thought I should thank you, Denise, I haven't felt so young in years. Now, what's the problem? Cuttlefish causing trouble? Another nomination?

This afternoon, huh, leaving it a bit late, aren't they? Are you sure he's a member? A she? And has she attended the required number of branch meetings to qualify? Well, who is it? Not poor old Mrs Gardiner, she's as mad as a cut snake! Who? Are you absolutely certain?

My sister! What?! You're not serious, are you? She's mad, I'll kill her, I'll break her bloody neck. Yes, alright, alright. I know. Calm? How can I be calm? What's she trying to do? Make a complete idiot of me? Don't answer that, Denise. She'll withdraw, I'll force her to.

People will turn to Cuttlefish; they won't take me seriously. Damage control? If I'll have to withdraw, I couldn't make a complete— You think so? Oh, oh, ohhh. Well, if you think we can still do it, if you think we'll still have the numbers. Right. If she stands, I've got to play it straight down the middle, huh huh. Well, I've established myself as a consensus man.

Kenny? I can't contact him. Look, he'll make all the difference, best fullback ever to play for the Panthers, terrific athlete, successful architect, designed the fountain in the mall, what more could you want?

Alright. I've settled down, how about a bite tonight? Discuss tactics. Around eight. Fine. The Wine Barrel. See you then.

ACT ONE

He hangs up.

Alright, Dot, now we'll see who's the clever dick.

SCENE EIGHT

MUM *and* KIM *relax after a hard day. Later that night.*

MUM: No note, no nothing. I'd have sworn there'd be some reaction.
KIM: Maybe he doesn't know yet.
MUM: I bet he knows, that Denise doesn't miss a trick.
KIM: I got those phone numbers.
MUM: Good. Finished typing the speech?
KIM: Yep.
MUM: She'll be able to read it now.
KIM: Look what I did at school.

She proudly displays a T-shirt which reads, 'DOT'S GOT THE LOT'.

MUM: Lovely.
KIM: Did it in Art. I'm gonna wear it at the meeting.
MUM: Good idea.

There is a roar outside. The sound of a big motorbike. Its headlights flash through the window.

My God! What's that?

The bike screeches to a halt.

KIM: Bikies! Might be Dingo's mates after revenge.
MUM: Revenge?
KIM: Remember that smoko? I borrowed it accidentally.

They arm themselves with brooms. A helmeted figure appears at the window.

MUM: Stay there, if you know what's good for you.

The figure opens the window and climbs in whilst MUM *belts it with a broom.*

Get out!
KIM: Don't think you can frighten us.
MUM: We're not scared of you.

The figure removes his helmet. It is KENNY. *Now overweight, bearded, with all the accoutrements of a biker.*

SONG: *'TO THE VALLEY UNKNOWN'*

KENNY: Thrown away the collar and tie
Ain't got no reason for stocks and shares to buy
Don't shave my face and I ain't got no place
Think of changin' my name to Ace

[*Chorus*] I'm gonna ride [ride] I'm gonna ride [ride]
I'm gonna ride [ride] to the valley unknown

I tell you family of a secret of mine
I never really did like that wife of mine
Something about her made me think she wasn't straight
My aim in life now is to put on weight

[*Chorus*] I'm gonna ride [ride] I'm gonna ride [ride]
I'm gonna ride [ride] to the valley unknown

And if I should be passing by
Save me a place at the table and some zucchini pie

Thrown away the collar and tie
Ain't got no reason for stocks and shares to buy
Don't shave my face and I ain't got no place
Think of changin' my name to Ace

[*Chorus*] I'm gonna ride [ride] I'm gonna ride [ride]
I'm gonna ride [ride] to the valley unknown
To the valley unknown
To the valley unknown
To the valley unknown.

END OF ACT ONE

ACT TWO

SCENE NINE

KENNY, MUM *and* KIM.

KENNY *sings a reprise of 'TO THE VALLEY UNKNOWN'*.

KENNY: I came here looking for sweet memories
And you've really made me feel at ease
Still it's good to be back, it's good to be here
I've come to eat your food and drink your beer

[*Chorus*] I'm gonna ride [ride] I'm gonna ride [ride]
I'm gonna ride [ride] to the valley unknown
To the valley unknown
To the valley unknown
To the valley unknown.

KENNY: Hi, gang! How's it going?
MUM: Kenny?
KENNY: Different?
MUM: What happened to you?
KENNY: Me?
MUM: Look at you …
KENNY: Good, eh?
MUM: Your hair …
KENNY: Yeah, I know, stress.
MUM: Stress?
KIM: Yeah, Mum, stress. It's a modern phenomenon, like RSI.
MUM: You poor thing.
KENNY: Hey, Ma, it's cool, I can handle it.
MUM: You've put on so much weight.
KENNY: Yeah, well …
KIM: It's alright for you, what about us? How embarrassing!

They hug.

Oh God, mind the beard, you look like Eric Grothe!

KENNY: Now hang on …
MUM: You look dreadful.
KENNY: Thanks, Ma, only took me six months to grow the bloody thing.
KIM: What happened to the suit and blow-wave?
KENNY: Time for a change.
KIM: There goes the media career.
KENNY: Tough.
MUM: Why haven't you written or phoned, we've been so worried about you.
KENNY: Take it easy, Ma.
KIM: What's with the bike?
KENNY: Freedom, sis.
KIM: What happened to the Commodore?
KENNY: Shit, it's hot, I'd kill for a cold one.
MUM: Quick, Kim, get yourself a beer.
KIM: Eh?
MUM: I mean, get your brother a beer.

She does.

KENNY: I rang before, but no-one was home. Called the old man at the office and left a message, but no reply. Where is he?
MUM: Scouting for votes.
KENNY: Votes?
MUM: Yes, he's standing for preselection.
KENNY: Far out!
KIM: Don't talk about it.
MUM: You can have a nice bath after, dear, and we'll fix your room.
KENNY: Don't worry, Ma, I'm not staying. Besides, I'm not into externals anymore, I'm into the soul.
MUM: The soul?
KENNY: Yeah, Ma.
MUM: Oh, my God.
KIM: Tell us the guts, what happened?
KENNY: Re-birth, re-discovery.
MUM: Yes?
KENNY: Sick of the goldfish bowl.
KIM: Really?

ACT TWO

KENNY: Yeah, I mean, a lifetime of doing the right thing, of being everyone's ... I dunno, hero. Out of control really.
MUM: Oh, yes. Didn't seem to mind at the time.
KENNY: That was then, this is now.
MUM: Right on, brother. And what caused this, this metamorphosis?
KENNY: I dunno, I just thought ...
MUM: Yes?
KENNY: I didn't like who I was.
MUM: Oh. I see. And Irene?
KENNY: Oh, her. Yeah, well, long story, really.
KIM: Tell.
KENNY: Well, basically, Irene ran off with Jeremy, and I thought, bugger this, got meself a bike, and pissed off to Alice.
MUM: Alice?
KIM: Who's Alice?
KENNY: Alice. The Centre. Alice Springs.
MUM: Irene left you?
KENNY: Well, sort of.
KIM: No wonder you've flipped.
KENNY: Apparently she'd been having it off with Jeremy before we even formed the partnership.
KIM: Told you she was a North Shore tart.
KENNY: So I sold him my share and zap! I'm outta there. Spent some time travelling around. All that Kerouac stuff.
MUM: Jack Kerouac! He was my generation.
KENNY: Got into Hunter S. Thompson as well, started doing my own thing in my own time.
MUM: I hate to say it, dear, but I think you're twenty years too late.
KENNY: Never look back, Ma.
MUM: Oh.
KENNY: Next step, down south.
MUM: Your father employs an image maker, and you find an image destroyer.
KENNY: Given up sport, too.
KIM: Oh, God! Not another hippy, brown rice and lentils, is it?
KENNY: Uh uh. McDonald's. Big Mac. I love 'em.

MUM: I hope you're not going to regret this, dear, it's awfully hard to lose weight once you've put it on, you know.
KENNY: Ma, I've had a lifetime of training, health food, diets, you name it. Now I'm gonna live a little.
MUM: Yes, I know, it's just that I'd hate to see you wake up one morning and wish you were back in Adelaide. Life has a funny way of throwing up little surprises, you know.
KENNY: Don't worry, Ma, I know where I'm goin' and that's the main thing.
MUM: Wait till your father sees you, he'll have a fit. He's—
KENNY: I tell ya, Ma, this is the life. You ought to try it.
MUM: Yes, I can just see myself driving around Australia on a motorbike.
KENNY: Hey! It's everyone's dream, and I'm doing it.

    A.D. *enters in a rush.*

A.D.: Hey, Kim, got that thing typed up for me yet? I need to check it over with Wacka. Now I'm off to the bowlo to see if we can't swing a few votes over a schooner or two. I've arranged to see Danny Maloney from the BLF, he hasn't got a hope of winning, so I might be able to persuade him to give me his preferences.
KIM: Guess who, A.D?
A.D.: Mmm? Hello there, jeez, Dingo didn't last long.
KIM: It's Kenny.
A.D.: Kenny?
KIM: Kenny.
A.D.: Kenny!

    A big hug.

Artie'll be pleased you've parked in the middle of his zucchinis, should make his day.
KENNY: How's it going, A.D?
A.D.: Never been better. You been away a long time.
KENNY: Yeah.
MUM: Aunt Dorothy's standing, too.
KENNY: Yeah, I can see that, Ma.
MUM: For preselection.
KENNY: Where, in Balmain?

ACT TWO

KIM: No, dummy, here.
KENNY: Against Dad?
A.D.: That's right.
KENNY: Holy shit, eh! Nothing like keeping it in the family.
KIM: Dad doesn't know yet.
KENNY: Oh, right …
A.D.: Hey, you can work for me.
KENNY: What?
A.D.: Campaign. I've got a lot of catching up to do.
KENNY: Not me, I'm off, hitting the bitumen, 'Fear and Loathing on the Road to Narooma'.
MUM: Your vocab's diminished, Kenny.
KENNY: Yeah? But I'm happy, Ma, so that's cool.

DAD enters, humming 'I'm In with the In Crowd'. He has blow-waved his hair and is snappily attired, an image maker has been to work on him.

KIM: You'll have to stay until the speeches.
MUM: Arthur!
DAD: What?
KIM: Dad?
DAD: What?
A.D.: Artie!
KENNY: Pa.
DAD: Pa?
MUM: Kenny.
DAD: What?
KIM: Kenny.
A.D.: It's Kenny.
KENNY: Great to see you, Pa.
DAD: Oh, my God.

He faints.

SCENE TEN

Later that night, the evening meal. MUM *is busily serving dinner.* DAD, KIM *and* KENNY *are eating.*

KENNY: Choko pickle! Thought I'd never see it again. Any zucchini pie?
MUM: No, everyone's so busy the garden seems to be neglected.
KENNY: I'll have a go at it, if you like.
MUM: Oh, would you? That'd be lovely, wouldn't it, dear?
DAD: Um, yes.
KIM: Dad, can I have some money for the excursion tomorrow? We're going into town.
DAD: No.
KIM: Only twenty bucks.
DAD: No.
KIM: Why not?
DAD: Because we can't afford it, that's why not.
MUM: Of course we can.
DAD: We cannot! I happen to have a campaign to run, in case you hadn't noticed.
MUM: We noticed, alright!
KENNY: Here you go, little sis, twenty big ones.

    KENNY *ostentatiously flicks her a twenty-dollar bill.*

KIM: Thanks, brother dear.
MUM: Arthur, I'll need some money to pay the house insurance.
DAD: It'll have to wait.
MUM: Oh, will it? What if there's a fire, or something?
DAD: We're talking about the future of this nation, that's why I'm standing. Not for personal gain, for the country, for Australia. We all have to make sacrifices.
MUM: Oh, do we? Well, I have my family to consider, and I'm not sacrificing them for anything.
DAD: It's the big picture that matters …

    A.D. *enters. She is done up to the nines. The family are stunned.*

KIM: Check it out.
KENNY: Wow, A.D.
MUM: Dorothy, you look …
DAD: Ridiculous.
MUM: Lovely.
A.D.: I have my image to consider.

ACT TWO

KENNY: Get you a cold one, A.D?
A.D.: No thank you, dear. I'm eschewing alcohol for the duration of the campaign. I may not see eye to eye with Hawke on everything, but I am following his example on this one. I owe it to my constituents.
DAD: The voters will never fall for that.
A.D.: You're a hypocrite, Arthur.
MUM: More corned meat, anyone?
A.D.: Kenny, I was wondering if you might like to accompany me down to the bowling club tonight? My shout.
KENNY: I'd—
DAD: If you don't mind, there are a few things I'd like to discuss with my son.
A.D.: But surely, Artie, you have a meeting with your campaign director this evening.
MUM: Yes, dear, wouldn't do to keep Denise waiting.
DAD: My campaign happens to be in very good shape, and I would like the opportunity to talk to my son.
A.D.: Well, I haven't the time to procrastinate. I've got an election to win.
MUM: You haven't eaten.

> A.D. *grabs a handful of food, hungrily tucking into it.*

A.D.: No time to let the grass grow, love.

> A.D. *exits hurriedly.*

MUM: Now look, Kenny …
KIM: I've got homework to do.
MUM: You can help me clean up first, young lady.
KIM: Oh yeah, okay, Mum.

> *They do.*

DAD: Now look, Kenny, about this, this way you're dressing and your hair and that beard … I mean you're, you're an embarrassment, son.
KENNY: Thanks a lot, Dad.
DAD: No, I mean it. I'm hosting an important party tomorrow night, and I don't want to give the wrong impression about us.
KENNY: Right. I'll remember that, Pa.
DAD: What's happened to you, son?
KENNY: Nothing, I just decided to do what I wanted to do.

DAD: Don't be absurd, no-one does what they want to do. Look, son. I've got a proposition to make.
KENNY: Sounds ominous.
DAD: I want to take you on the campaign trail with me.
KENNY: So does A.D.
DAD: Your aunt's a lunatic, we all know that. Now, her standing is proving to be a bloody embarrassment, but Denise ...
KENNY: Ha!
DAD: My campaign manager, Denise, reckons that if you were to be seen at my side, I'd be damn near unbeatable. People have got long memories around here, Kenny, I'll get every vote from the football club if you're with me. There are about fifteen members from there, and that'd ensure me a win, even if your mad aunt stands.
KENNY: I don't want to sound bipartisan, Father, but you don't seem to understand. I'm not the person I was.
DAD: Of course, you'll need to clean yourself up a bit. Got to fly. Don't forget what I said, I'm relying on you.

> DAD *goes to leave, then returns with an afterthought.*

Oh, great to see you home, boy.

> DAD *exits, leaving a stunned* KENNY.

KENNY: I need some space, this place's madder than Alice.

> *He exits 'to find some space'.*

SONG: *'THERE'S TOO MUCH UNSAID'*

MUM: Between a rock and a hard place
That's what it seems like here nowadays

What with Kenny and Irene split
There must be pain because of it
Though I see ... he shows not a sign
And I fear ... there's too much unsaid

And what my husband is playing at
He's at the crease, though he's lost his bat
Could it be ... lost virility?

ACT TWO

But I fear ... there's too much unsaid

Between a rock and a hard place
That's what it seems like here nowadays

A family torn, yet on the same side
Caught in the middle and nowhere to hide
I don't know ... where my support should lie
And I fear ... there's too much unsaid

Between a rock and a hard place
That's what it seems like here nowadays
Between a rock and a hard place
That's what it seems like here nowadays.

SCENE ELEVEN

At home, the party is in full swing. Outside can be seen the silhouetted figures of the partygoers. There is a lot of chat and laughter. Discreet music. From time to time, a loud male voice can be heard, breaking out above the general hubbub.

MUM *and* A.D. *are inside, preparing salads, etc.*

A.D.: Have a go at him, will you, carrying on like a pork chop. Who does he think he is?

MUM: He does seem very pleased with himself.

A.D.: He'll keep.

    DAD *pokes his head around the corner. The cat who got the cream.*

DAD: Fabulous! How's the salads going? Marvellous idea, darling, everyone's having a ball. Couldn't have wished for a better turnout. Oh, you're still here are you, Dot? Thought you'd be out campaigning!

A.D.: Oh, good, someone to slice the onions.

DAD: Any nibblies?

    MUM *hands* DAD *a plate of snacks.*

Thanks, love. Oh, the dress looks ... terrific.

    He disappears.

MUM: See if we need any more drinks, please, Dot?

A.D.: Do I—?
MUM: Please.

> A.D. *exits reluctantly, and is almost bowled over by* KENNY, *looking a little neater.*

KENNY: I don't believe it; this guy was telling me he wanted to ban unions. A Labor supporter wanting to ban trade unions? What's going down, Ma?
MUM: Don't you read the papers?
KENNY: Oh, shit no. Not since I hit the road. The media is just a tool for the perpetuation of materialistic values.
MUM: Really?
KENNY: Yeah.
MUM: Take this out, please, dear.

> *She hands him another plate of nibblies.*

It's all so simple, isn't it?

> KIM *rushes in, nearly colliding with* KENNY.

KIM: Mum, this guy, what a spunk … you should hear him talk. He's so smart. And he looks so cool. Gawd, makes Spud look like a chip. You should see his car.
MUM: Holden?
KIM: No way, Saab. Totally computerised.
MUM: What's he do?
KIM: Lawyer. Suing Greenpeace. Any more beer?

> A.D. *bowls in. She carries an armload of wine bottles.*

A.D.: Look at this. Chardonnay! Strike me dead, what's the world coming to?
KIM: Mum! Any more beer? Dad told me to hurry.
A.D.: Only light, of course!
MUM: What's your lawyer drink?
KIM: Perrier, what ya reckon?
MUM: How sensible.

> KENNY *re-enters.*

KENNY: What's W.A. Inc.?
MUM: In the fridge.
A.D.: I need a real drink.

ACT TWO

KIM: Oh no, don't, A.D. Think of your followers.

MUM: Kim! In the fridge, there's some gherkin paté, that should keep them quiet for a while.

KIM: Okay, Mum.

A.D.: And the beer.

KIM: Perrier!

A.D.: Soda's good enough for the likes of him.

    KIM *rushes outside.* KENNY *observes the party.*

KENNY: This's out of it, Ma. How can you put up with it? I can't work out where these dudes are coming from.

MUM: Pardon?

KENNY: How come the Left supported Hawke?

A.D.: Ancient history.

KENNY: Yeah, but … he was their sworn enemy, ever since uranium mining was an issue.

MUM: Didn't do him much good in the long run, did it?

KENNY: They dumped him …

A.D.: Kenny! The cobwebs are beginning to clear.

MUM: He's not coming back to us, is he, Dot?

KENNY: How can Labor voters support media monopolies?

A.D.: It's called expediency.

KENNY: And, and Hawke retiring from parliament on TV …

MUM: *That's* called repaying your debts.

A.D.: I'd have called it tacky.

KENNY: And Whitlam teams with Fraser? Something very weird is going down here.

MUM: God, Dot, I can see the wheels starting to turn. He's not brain dead, after all.

KENNY: Economic rationalism? What happened to idealism?

A.D.: Dirty word.

KENNY: It's got me stuffed, I tell ya. Who represents the battlers if we've joined the—?

MUM: *We've?!*

KENNY: I mean, they've—

MUM: Careful, darling, you're starting to sound like you've got a modicum of intelligence.

KENNY: Hey, cool it, Ma. Just an observation, doesn't mean I'm gonna get sucked back into this, this materialistic nonsense. No way, I mean, if ever I needed reinforcement, well, this is it. It's the personal journey that really matters.

    DAD *appears around the corner (or through the window).*

DAD: Kim, Kenny, come on, hurry up, there's some people I want you to meet. You're in big demand, you know.

KENNY: Okay, Pa.

DAD: Quick sticks.

    KENNY *obeys as* DAD *goes.*

SONG: 'TOE THE PARTY LINE'

A.D.: Well you know I worry about that brother of mine
Take a look at him now, he's drinking summer wine
Greasing up to the posers
Let's get to the club before it closes

MUM: I don't know why I agreed to this
Who are these fools he's out to impress?
He promised me there'd be dancing
He's like a boil that needs lancing

MUM / A.D.: [*chorus*] So let's drink another wine
And toe the party line
'N' get plastered ... blastered
So let's drink another wine
And toe the party line
'N' get plastered ... blastered

A.D.: Why can't we leave the bastards here to discuss politics?
Take a trip to the club and have a few nips
A gay old time on the pokies
It's gotta be a better way to go

MUM / A.D.: [*chorus*] So let's drink another wine
And toe the party line
'N' get plastered ... blastered
So let's drink another wine

ACT TWO

	And toe the party line 'N' get plastered ... blastered
A.D.:	Pardon me sir, a dry white wine for you sir?
MUM:	A nightmare in your home, they're all just clones

MUM / A.D.: [*chorus*] So let's drink another wine
And toe the party line
'N' get plastered ... blastered
So let's drink another wine
And toe the party line
'N' get plastered ... blastered
So let's drink another wine
And toe the party line
'N' get plastered ... blastered.

As the song ends, KIM *enters to address the audience.*

KIM: I got really pissed off. I mean, after a while all this election stuff was getting out of control. The family was going completely over the top about it.

It was good to have Kenny home again. We were getting on really well. Yeah, well, he did lend me a few bucks, so I had to be nice to him.

It was unreal though, the place was like a mad house with all the comings and goings and the plotting. Secret phone calls, in the dark, clandestine meetings everywhere, pretty cool word, heh, clandestine. It was wild.

One thing, though, I decided to work really hard at school. I knew, then and there, I had to get out of the place the minute I finished Year Twelve. I had to get out into the world and make my mark, but I reckon if you're gonna beat men at their own game, you're gonna need some pretty good ammunition. I mean, check out Mum, and A.D. for that matter. They really impressed me the way they stood up to Dad. Eh, sisters!

No man's gonna walk over this lady. No way. That's what appeals to me about politics. Power. I'd love to have a guy running around, doing my typing and stuff. It wouldn't be Spud though, he can't spell.

SCENE TWELVE

The big meeting. DAD *and* A.D. *are to give their campaign speeches to the local branch members.* KENNY *strides to the lectern. He has cleaned up, but the beard is still there, his hair trendily tied in a ponytail.*

KENNY: Thank you, Rod. You know, I played juniors with Simon Cuttlefish. Not a bad player, till he signed with Manly, that is!

   Laughter.

Anyway, a stimulating address, one which will give us all plenty to think about. It now gives me tremendous pleasure to introduce a man who really needs no introduction, my father, Mr Arthur Green.

   Applause.

DAD: Brothers and sisters, this is a moment I have long dreamt of, the moment I address my local branch, seeking your support to contest an election representing this great party. Imagine, then, the pride I feel having my son, Kenny Green, introduce me. Thank you, Kenny.

Brothers and sisters, this is a time when we must all make genuine sacrifices to serve our fellow man. We live in a world of turmoil. In an age of uncertainty. Those things we once held as solid and secure are now at risk. We have to make critical choices. We are not simply choosing between Rodney and I, or Danny Maloney and I, or even my sister and I. Oh, no. The ramifications are far wider, the winner of this ballot must take to Canberra a commitment and dedication which will test even the strongest of souls.

Whoever this meeting chooses will be going to Canberra to serve the Australian Labor Party. To represent the men and women of the Australian Labor Party, and ipso facto, the whole of Australia.

This is an historic Labor government, one which has survived. One which has learnt to grow and adapt. To adapt to the needs of the electorate. A united Labor Party.

Now, I agree with Rod that we need reform, but I caution, hasten slowly. There is a time for idealism, but it isn't now. This is time for consolidation. Social reform cannot be allowed to obstruct economic reform, for without economic reform, there can be no social reform.

ACT TWO

This is a time to get the house in order, to keep the ship on an even keel, the playing field level, and the goalposts in the one spot.

Our party is one with traditional values. We are all members of a large, extended family, and the family is the key to a progressive, stable and harmonious society. I believe we must be sympathetic to those who, for whatever reason, lose the way. We must be forgiving.

You all know my sister is also standing for preselection. And why shouldn't she? This is a democracy, and I welcome anyone who wishes to throw their hat into the ring, as long as their determination is to serve, soberly.

But, dear friends, keep it in the family. That's the key to our success as a party. The family is the core, remove the core, and you have no heart.

It's all very well to argue for reforms, Danny. All of them are worthwhile, but we must be able to pay for them. To do this, we must win and maintain the support of the business community. Without their support, there can be no economic recovery, and without that, we're all gone.

Now, I believe, um, I believe …

He fumbles through his notes.

Yes, ah … people are more important than trees. They are more important than rocks and dirt. Don't get me wrong, I'm a great nature lover, but I put people first. My priority is to improve the lot of all the people and to serve this electorate.

Now, I will prove myself to be a reliable, dedicated Member. One who will keep the Australian Labor Party in government. In Canberra. In control. In power.

Thank you, all. Thank you, Kenny, for coming all the way from Adelaide to introduce your dad, and God bless Australia.

Applause. KENNY *stands and joins* DAD, *shaking his hand.* DAD *goes to leave the podium, when he realises that* KENNY *is about to speak.*

KENNY: Thank you to Mr Arthur Green.

DAD *waits, smiling expectantly.*

As you all know, there are two members from the Green family contesting this ballot. I felt that if I was to introduce my father, then it would only be fair that I should also introduce my aunt.

This is not what DAD *expected. He tries to intervene, but realises that this would be politically embarrassing. He leaves the podium with as much dignity as he can manage, which isn't much.*

And so it is with much pleasure that I introduce a lady who refuses to lie down, my Aunt Dorothy.

Applause and some laughter.

A.D.: I started out in this campaign really as a bit of a joke. To get up the nose of another candidate, if you know what I mean. Well, bugger it. It isn't a joke anymore. I'm sick to death of the way this party's going. What these people are doing is taking the Labor out of the Labor Party. You all know that, and I am certain of it. I got a phone call the other night asking me to withdraw. You know where it came from? The Federal bloody Executive, and you don't have to be Einstein to work out which powerbroker initiated it. I told him to get stuffed. He made a few threats, and I laughed at him.

You see, you can't buy what I stand for. I stand for the Australian Labor People, and the movement that grew out of the oppression of the working man and woman. I care about the future. I care for more than economics; I think there is more to life than economic rationalism. I think there is a lot wrong with this country, and by ignoring the poor, the sick, and the needy, we are creating an underclass that will never get a fair go. I know what you'll say, you'll say I'm bloody naive. Well, I won't be changing me mind on the strength of an opinion poll. Now, I've cut out the grog and I won't be dining out with the Double Bay set. No way.

You know what I'd like to see? I'd like to see someone relight the Light on the Hill. I'd like us to have a bloody go for the sake of all Australians, not just the rich and powerful. Vote for me, and you'll get no bullshit and plenty of hard work.

SONG: 'ODE TO THE PARTY'

A.D.:   I joined the Labor Party in nineteen forty-three
           I knew what I was fighting for, things I wanted to see

ACT TWO

        A fair deal, a just deal, for those like you and me
        To stand up for our rights and our identity

A.D. / MUM / KIM: [*chorus*]
        So brothers and sisters, join in the fight
        So long as there's injustice, we will have the right
        To march, to shout, to let our grievance ring
        If we all believe the world is for saving

A.D.:   The party's been alive now since eighteen ninety-one
        Would the founding fathers be pleased with what we've done?
        We've battles won, we've battles lost, we've battles just begun
        So long as we're united, the battles can be won

A.D. / MUM / KIM: [*chorus*]
        So brothers and sisters, join in the fight
        So long as there's injustice, we will have the right
        To march, to shout, to let our grievance ring
        If we all believe the world is for saving
        So brothers and sisters, join in the fight
        So long as there's injustice, we will have the right
        To march, to shout, to let our grievance ring
        If we all believe the world is for saving.

SCENE THIRTEEN

MUM, KENNY *and* KIM *sit in front of the TV.*

KENNY: Don't know how you can watch this stuff.
KIM: Well, you either drink, smoke, or watch TV. All mind-altering substances.
KENNY: Mind-numbing, you mean.
MUM: Quiet! I'm trying to hear.
KIM: Alright, Mum. No need to be so touchy.
MUM: Just be quiet!

    Silence.

    DAD *enters, he has been gardening.*

DAD: Absolute disgrace that garden, absolute disgrace.
MUM: I've never seen it look worse.

DAD: Overgrown with weeds, hardly a zucchini left, whole thing's a bloody disaster. I'll need to completely dig it up and start again. Someone's even backed over the silverbeet! If you can't grow silverbeet, you can't grow anything!
KENNY: 'Fraid that was me, Pa.
DAD: Wouldn't surprise me.

    KENNY *turns off the TV.*

MUM: What on earth are you doing? I'm watching 'Spin for Your Luck'.
KIM: Come off it, Mum, you hate that show.
MUM: I don't, I just hate the compere.
KENNY: Look, I know you're shitty with me.
DAD: Why? Why would I be shitty, just because you betrayed me?
MUM: Don't be so melodramatic, Arthur.
DAD: Well, he did. How was I to know he was going to introduce her too? Made me look like a complete idiot.
KIM: At least he washed his hair.
KENNY: I'm sorry, Pa, but I couldn't do anything else. Anyway, I'm going to hit the frog.
MUM: Frog?
KENNY: Frog.
KIM: Frog and toad. Road.
MUM: So soon?
KENNY: Yeah, reckon I've wreaked enough havoc around here. Time to burn up the bitumen.
MUM: 'Burn up the bitumen', oh really?
DAD: So, you're just going to ride around the place, wasting your life?
KENNY: I wouldn't say wasting.
KIM: Just being hip, eh?
KENNY: That's where I want to be right now. Hey, why don't you come with me?
KIM: No way, José. I have no desire to drop out of this game. In fact, watching that Denise operate, I've decided to slog my guts out so I can do a uni degree and get a job with the party.
DAD: What's Denise got to do with it?
KIM: Power over men.
MUM: What, no more Spud and Dingo?

ACT TWO

KIM: No time. Upwardly mobile chick, that's me.
KENNY: Very groovy!
KIM: Oh, and I'm on to you too, brother dear!
KENNY: Eh?
KIM: You haven't dropped out at all, have you?
KENNY: I haven't necessarily 'dropped out', but I'm certainly into 'alternate lifestyles'.
KIM: Oh, yeah? What about 'The Big Wombat'?
KENNY: How'd you—?
MUM: Big Wombat? What's that?
KIM: It's a motel in Alice Springs. In the shape of a wombat.
MUM: A wombat?
KIM: Yeah, can you believe it? Tacky, or what?
DAD: So?
KIM: Jack Kerouac here designed it.
DAD: Kenny?
KIM: Uh huh.
DAD: You mean to say you haven't completely given up on architecture?
KENNY: Well, you know, from time to time, Pa, a man's gotta eat.
KIM: You're just like everyone else, absolutely full of shit.
MUM: Kim!
KIM: Well, just because Irene gave him the flick doesn't mean he has to throw in the towel completely. The superstar's so used to winning that once he drops a game he tosses it all in.
MUM: Don't be too harsh, darling. Marriage break-ups sometimes have a strange effect on people, be a bit sensitive.
KENNY: Yeah.
DAD: Yeah.
KIM: Okay, look boys, I'm sorry.
KENNY: It's cool. I can handle it.

    A.D. *rushes in.*

A.D.: Anyone ring for me?
DAD: No. If they did, I would have told them you were out.
MUM: Kenny's heading off.
A.D.: Oh, is he?
KENNY: Yeah, Hunter S. Thompson awaits, A.D.

A.D.: You can't run away like that.
KENNY: Who's running away?
DAD: You are.
A.D.: No he's not.
KENNY: Eh?
A.D.: You're going nowhere, my boy.
KENNY: Take it easy, A.D.
A.D.: Take it easy?! I've been running around like a chook with me head cut off, and he tells me to 'Take it easy'!
MUM: What's up, Dot?
A.D.: They've discovered an irregularity in the voting.
ALL: What?
A.D.: A whole batch of voters hadn't signed on, their names didn't show in the records as having attended enough meetings to qualify.
MUM: Oh, Lord, no! Don't tell me we'll have to go through this all again?
A.D.: In a sense, yes, we will, I hope.
DAD: Well, you can count me out. I couldn't stand the embarrassment.
KIM: So, what's the story?
A.D.: Mr Cuttlefish will have to stand down. They'll be calling for the nominations again.
KIM: If Dad's going to pull out, you might get up this time, A.D.
A.D.: Not on your nelly.
DAD: If you hadn't got involved in the first place, none of this would have happened. I lost votes because of you.
A.D.: You lost votes because Denise did a deal on behalf of the Left.
DAD: I know that, so?
A.D.: Danny Maloney withdrew when he discovered his votes had been directed to Cuttlefish.
DAD: Right.
A.D.: No, he's the Left. Danny's a man of principle.
KENNY: So Pa's votes went to Cuttlefish because the Left and the Right did a deal. Right?
A.D.: Right! All orchestrated by Denise.
KIM: I've got to get into this.
MUM: Let me get this straight. Danny Maloney withdraws, Dad expects his votes to go to him.

ACT TWO

ALL: Right.
MUM: But Denise and Cuttlefish have done a deal, whereby Maloney's supporters switch to Cuttlefish.
ALL: Right.
A.D.: No, he's the Left.
MUM: Well, whatever. So, your votes are split between Dad and Cuttlefish.
A.D.: And Cuttlefish wins.
ALL: Right.
A.D.: But some of Maloney's votes aren't legal, thus a recount.
DAD: What a bloody mess.
MUM: So what now?
A.D.: Kenny stands.
KENNY: What?
A.D.: Oh look, it's perfect. The party needs a candidate who can deflect the flak from this debacle. Who would be better? Who has already proved himself to be bipartisan? Who is the one to unite the party?
KIM: Kenny?
A.D.: Kenny.
ALL: Kenny!
KENNY: No!
A.D.: I'm waiting for a call from the Federal Executive.
KENNY: Excuse me …
A.D.: Excuse me! Denise has been given the boot, you're looking at the new branch secretary.
MUM: Well done, Dot!
A.D.: And I'm going to need an offsider, Kath?
MUM: Me?
A.D.: You.
KIM: I've *gotta* get into this!
A.D.: Of course, Kenny will need a campaign manager, someone to guide him through the minefield, to introduce him at public rallies, to help formulate policy.
DAD: Well …
A.D.: I thought you'd be ideal, Arthur.
DAD: I could have my arm twisted. I suppose he'll need someone with expertise …

KENNY: Now hang on here, I'm not getting railroaded into this. No way. I've seen enough in the last few days to convince me that I've chosen the right path. Freedom, that's what it's all about.

A.D.: Oh, come on, Kenny ...

KENNY: No, A.D. Absolutely not. I'm not prepared to play the games necessary to make it in politics. Not the way things are now. I was brought up to believe in integrity. I don't see a lot of that in today's politician.

MUM: That's my boy, you sound much better when you talk like a human being.

A.D.: Doesn't he?!

KENNY: Well, what's the point? The parties pinch each other's policies, they constantly backtrack as soon as the wind changes, I mean, you might as well run the country on opinion polls. I was ready to man the barricades in seventy-five—

KIM: Person.

KENNY: Eh?

KIM: Person the barricades. Man is sexist.

KENNY: Kim, please! We all had something to believe in then. Gough set an agenda and we believed in it. God, even though we didn't like Fraser, at least we knew where we stood with him.

A.D.: And now?

KENNY: Now? It's hopeless, isn't it? GST, Fightback, One Nation ... unemployment over ten per cent and rising, kids on the streets, social division, who's addressing these problems?

DAD: Well said, lad. Your grandfather would have been proud of you.

KENNY: I mean, I might be interested if I still thought the party stood for something, but I'm afraid The Light on the Hill's gone out.

DAD: Don't you see, son, you could be the one to relight it.

KENNY: Listen, family. It's a touching thought, but the world awaits ...

DAD: You've got charisma, boy.

A.D.: And integrity.

MUM: And a brain.

KIM: And a great sister ...

KENNY: In the immortal words of Jeff Fenech, 'I love youse all', but I gotta split.

The phone rings. KIM *answers.*

ACT TWO

KIM: [*on the phone*] Hello? Just a minute. [*To* KENNY] Kenny, it's for you. It's—

KENNY: I'm not going to be dragooned—

> *He takes the phone.*
>
> [*On the phone*] Hello? Yes, yes sir, yes sir, yes *sir*.
>
> *The photo of Ben Chifley is illuminated.*

SONG: 'ALL I CAN DO, I'LL DO FOR YOU'

KENNY: It was like the sun rising within me
Though a veil had been lifted from my eyes
It was like the moon had lodged within my throat
Though a drawbridge had been lowered across the moat
It was like the earth had sprouted forth zucchinis
To feed all the needy people of the world.

ALL: It was like the sun rising within him
Though a veil had been lifted from his eyes
It was like the stars had all spelled out his name
Though a drought had given way to rain
It was like the earth had sprouted forth zucchinis
To feed all the needy people of the world.

KIM: [*spoken*] My God, who was that on the phone?

KENNY: [*sung*] I tell you it was him h h h h h h him
I tell you it was h h h h h h him
And he said Kenny Kenny Kenny I want you to stand
And I said all I can do, I'll do for you
Now I may not be a Panther anymore
And I may not be an architect that's for sure
But there is one thing Chif wishes me to be
He wants me to be be be be be, a Labor MP

ALL: I tell you it was him h h h h h h him
I tell you it was h h h h h h him
And he said Kenny Kenny Kenny I want you to stand
And I said all I can do, I'll do for you

DAD: I'm so proud of you my son and heir

MUM:	And I can't wait to see you on 'A Current Affair'
A.D.:	Let's drink a toast for the sake of it
KIM:	And if you go overseas, I wouldn't mind a trip
ALL:	It was like the sun rising within him
	Though a veil had been lifted from his eyes
	It was like the earth had sprouted forth zucchinis
	To feed all the needy people of the world
	It was like the earth had sprouted forth zucchinis
	To feed all the needy people of the world

KIM: [*spoken*] So, there you go. He absolutely romped it in. Increased the majority.

Well, I reckon if Kenny can do it, so can I. I mean, you gotta be in it to win it. I'm doing Pol Sci at uni, am President of the Students' Union, and President of the Labor Club.

And, of course you know who my inspiration is …

She points to the flashing Ben Chifley.

He's my man. Yeah, they don't make 'em like him anymore.

THE END

www.ingramcontent.com/pod-product-compliance
Lightning Source LLC
Chambersburg PA
CBHW050025090426
42734CB00021B/3420